Ripley's
Believe It or Not!®

WEIRD-ITIES!

Publisher Anne Marshall
Editorial Director Rebecca Miles
Assistant Editor Charlotte Howell
Text Geoff Tibballs
Proofreader Judy Barratt
Picture Researchers James Proud, Charlotte Howell
Art Director Sam South
Senior Designer Michelle Foster
Reprographics Juice Creative

Executive Vice President Norm Deska
Vice President, Archives and Exhibits Edward Meyer

PUBLISHER'S NOTE

While every effort has been made to verify the accuracy of the entries in this book, the Publishers cannot be held responsible for any errors contained in the work. They would be glad to receive any information from readers.

WARNING

Some of the stunts and activities in this book are undertaken by experts and should not be attempted by anyone without adequate training and supervision.

Published by Ripley Publishing 2013
Ripley Publishing, Suite 188, 7576 Kingspointe Parkway,
Orlando, Florida 32819, USA

2 4 6 8 10 9 7 5 3 1

ISBN 978-1-60991-023-5

Some of this material first appeared in *Ripley's Believe It or Not!*
Expect... The Unexpected

Library of Congress Cataloging-in-Publication data is available

Manufactured in China in February/2013 by Leo Paper
1st printing

Ripley's Believe It or Not!

WEIRD-ITIES!

AMAZING ANIMALS

Ripley
PUBLISHING
a Jim Pattison Company

PAGE
9
PAGE
28

AMAZING ANIMALS

Curious critters. If you think people are astounding, you haven't met these incredible creatures! Discover the potty pig Olympics, the tiny 50-cm (20-in) horse, and the ugliest dog you have ever seen!

PAGE 33

PAGE 34

WEB OF INTRIGUE

Instead of using traditional canvases, Enrique Ramos, of Mexico City, known as "The Fly Guy," creates tiny portraits of famous people on flies, feathers, beans, animal bones, and even bats!

Marlon Brando painted on a quails egg, measuring only 1 in (2.5 cm) high.

Without the help of any kind of magnification, Ramos has handpainted Da Vinci's "*Mona Lisa*" on a bird feather, a bean, and a stuffed bat. Often his pictures take under two minutes. He has even painted seven faces on a single human hair!

Sometimes Ramos uses no paint at all. He made a portrait of The Beatles from more than 60 dung beetles and hundreds of butterfly wings, and a bust of Abraham Lincoln from the hair of his son and daughter.

Ramos likes to paint subjects on real cobwebs too. He is unable to correct mistakes and also considers himself lucky if one-third of the gathered webs survive to form one of his cobweb paintings.

This bat was created to celebrate Halloween and the Mexican Day of the Dead festival and depicts Freddy Krueger from Nightmare on Elm Street, Lon Chaney as the Wolfman, and Bela Lugosi as Dracula.

A depiction of Spiderman—one of Ramos's most recent works—is made from nearly 20 lb (9 kg) of large wolf spiderwebs, and stands more than 2 ft (60 cm) in height.

These butterflies are part of a 35-piece Mexican history series. The first shows the Spanish conquistador, Hernando Cortez, and the second depicts the tragic Aztec-Mayan love story of Popoca and Miztla.

DUCK DIALECTS

It sounds quackers, but an English scientist has discovered that ducks have regional accents. Ducks in London are noisier than those in rural Cornwall as they have to raise their voices to compete with traffic.

GOLF-BALL GUZZLER

Doctors in England removed 28 golf balls from the stomach of a German shepherd who frequently takes walks along a golf course with his owner.

VANISHING ACT

Seven years after mysteriously disappearing, Ewok, a nine-year-old Shih Tzu, suddenly returned to Crofton, British Columbia, home of Jim and Barbara Reed in 2001.

BARKING MATH

Alissa Nelson, of Urbandale, Iowa, has a mongrel named Oscar who can do math addition problems. He answers a variety of mathematical sums by barking. For example, when asked the sum of two and two, he responds with four barks.

INHERITANCE KITTY

In the 1960s, San Diego doctor William Grier left his entire fortune of $415,000 to his two 15-year-old cats, Brownie and Hellcat.

SURVIVED FALL

Andy, a cat owned by Florida senator Ken Myer, fell 16 floors (200 ft/61 m) from a building in the 1970s—and survived!

THE YAP OF LUXURY

Dudley's bakery, in Fort Myers, Florida, is a dog's dream come true. Created by Vickie Emmanuele, the bakery offers specially made fancy gourmet treats and dog cakes.

DOG'S HOME

As a reward for the dog saving her from a 2001 house fire, actress Drew Barrymore placed her $3-million Beverly Hills home in trust with her golden labrador Flossie so that it would always have a roof over its head.

FEELING SLUGISH

These sea slugs certainly stand out from the crowd. They are called nudibranchs, and they get their venom and stings from the food they eat, which includes poisonous corals, sea sponges, and sea anemones. Nudibranchs wear bright colors to advertise their toxic skin to predators.

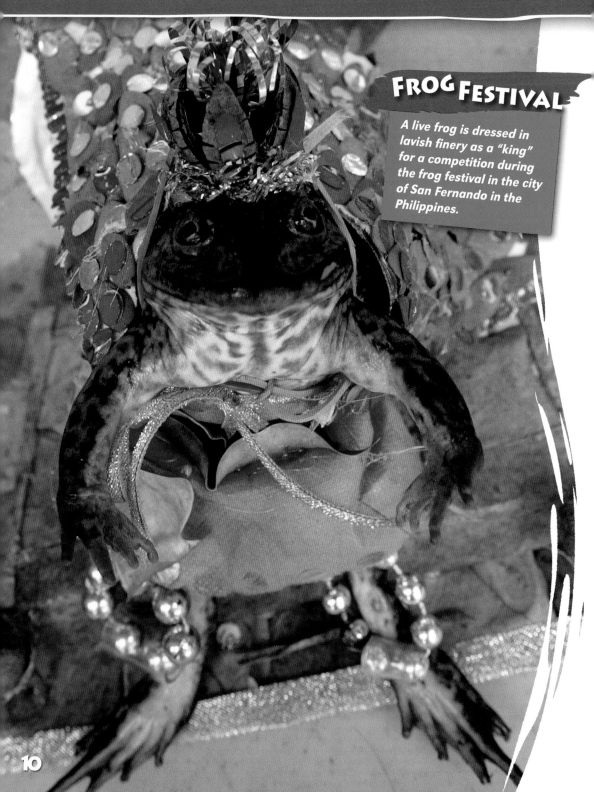

FROG FESTIVAL

A live frog is dressed in lavish finery as a "king" for a competition during the frog festival in the city of San Fernando in the Philippines.

CANINE CANDIDATE

In a bid to add color to the 2002 French presidential campaign, and to warn politicians against complacency, Serge Scotto tried to enter the name of his dog Saucisse as a rival candidate. But despite picking up over four percent of the vote in municipal elections in Marseille, Saucisse failed to obtain the necessary backing to oppose Jacques Chirac in the final stages of the presidential election.

EXPERT WITNESS

A police dog took the stand in a Pittsburgh, Pennsylvania, courtroom in 1994. The defense attorney tried to prove that the dog, not his client, was the aggressor in a fight.

PUNCH-DRUNK

A black bear in Baker Lake, Washington, was found passed out on a resort lawn. He got that way after stealing and drinking 36 cans of campers' beer!

GONE IN A FLASH

A single lightning strike on a farm in northern Israel killed an incredible 10,000 chickens.

HIGH MARKING

Giant pandas mark their territory by performing a handstand and urinating as high as possible up the side of a tree!

LOST AND FOUND

A dog that had been reported missing from his home in Columbus, Ohio, in 2002 turned up inside a 10-ft (3-m) long python that was found lurking under a neighbor's house. The neighbor called the police when she spotted the large snake with an ominous bulge in its middle.

HOLY CAT

Mike McGregor, from Edinburgh, Scotland, had never spotted anything unusual about the markings of his pet cat Brandy, until he saw Christ's face, just as it appears on the Turin Shroud, staring out at him. He said: "It's not every day that you see the face of Jesus in your cat's fur."

COW HIDE

It takes an incredible 3,000 cows to supply the National Football League with enough leather for just one season's worth of footballs!

FIRST CLASS HAMSTER

Emptying a mail box in Cambridge, England, one day, mailman Robert Maher was stunned to see a hamster peeping out from an envelope marked "Do Not Bend." He took it to veterinary surgeon Patrick von Heimendahl, who said that the animal—nicknamed First Class—was lucky to be alive. The hamster, thought to be about a year old, had miraculously survived a journey through the postal system.

UNUSUAL PASSENGER

When a man rides a bike, it's nothing special, but when a dog rides a man who rides a bike, that is special! The dog is Spike, a Jack Russell terrier, who can be seen perched on the shoulders of his owner, Denton Walthall, as the latter cycles around the streets of Henrico, Virginia. Mr. Walthall explained how the unusual pose started: "One day I was calling him and he came running at a fast pace. I was squatting down to catch him but he flew up, landed on my leg and then scrambled up on my shoulder. And he was at home. Sometimes I try to get him down, but he simply positions himself further on my back so that he can stay there."

CATTLE WEDDING

In July 2005, a pair of dwarf Brahman cattle were married in a lavish Thai wedding ceremony. Krachang Kanokprasert, the owner of the bull, originally wanted to buy the bride, but when her owner refused to sell, the two farmers agreed to join the miniature breeding stock in matrimony.

MIGHTY PLUNGE

Sam, a German shepherd with California's Lodi Police Department, jumped 50 ft (15 m) into a river from a bridge while pursuing a suspect in 2001. Once in the water, Sam swam after the suspect and proceeded to herd him to his human colleagues.

ACTIVE ANTS

An ant colony built beneath Melbourne, Australia, in 2004 measured a staggering 60 mi (97 km) wide. The Argentine ants formed a giant supercolony as a result of co-operative behavior.

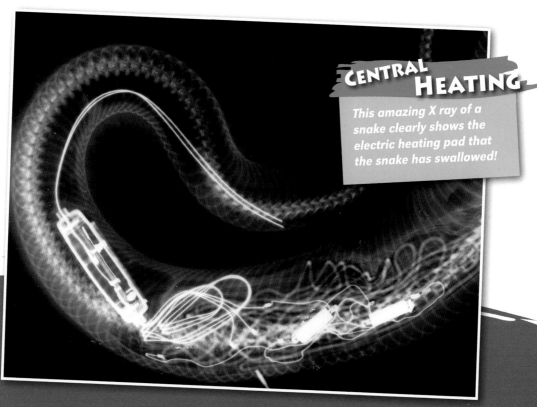

CENTRAL HEATING

This amazing X ray of a snake clearly shows the electric heating pad that the snake has swallowed!

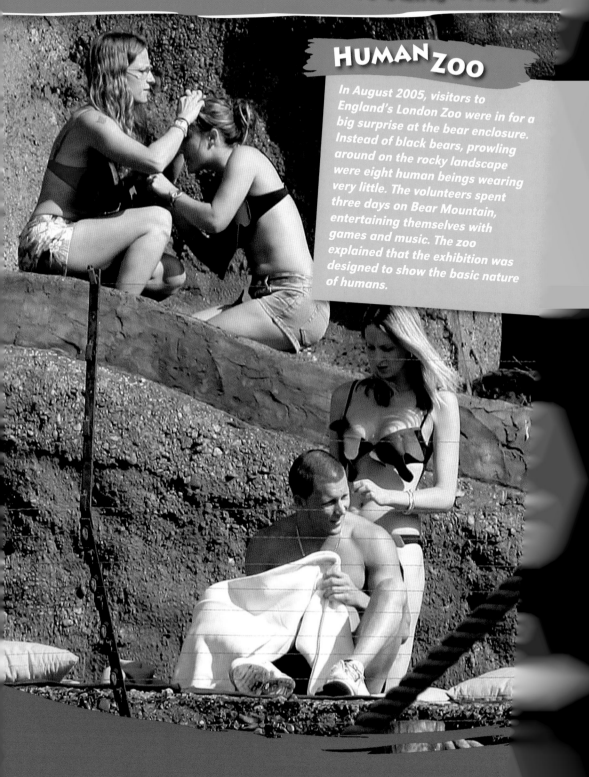

HUMAN ZOO

In August 2005, visitors to England's London Zoo were in for a big surprise at the bear enclosure. Instead of black bears, prowling around on the rocky landscape were eight human beings wearing very little. The volunteers spent three days on Bear Mountain, entertaining themselves with games and music. The zoo explained that the exhibition was designed to show the basic nature of humans.

GREAT ESCAPE

Who let the dogs out? That's exactly what staff at Battersea Dogs' Home in London, England, wanted to know.

In 2004, several mornings in a row, staff arrived at Battersea Dogs' Home to find that as many as nine dogs had escaped from their compounds and were causing chaos in the kitchen. In a bid to solve the mystery of how the dogs managed to get free, the dogs' home installed video surveillance cameras. These revealed that a three-year-old Lurcher called Red had learned how not only to unbolt his own kennel door using his nose and teeth, but also how to to free his fellow hounds to join in the adventure, helping themselves to food in the kitchen.

Having studied how staff moved the bolt to unlock the kennel door, Red the lurcher used his teeth to do the same.

Please make sure my kennel door is always locked – I can open them!

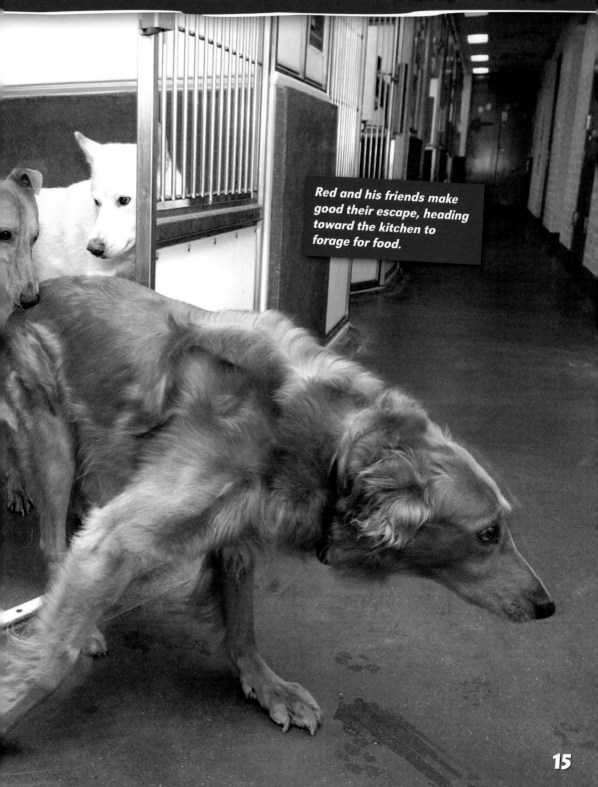

Red and his friends make good their escape, heading toward the kitchen to forage for food.

GREEN BEARS

In 2004, the usually white coats of Sheba and her son Inuka, Singapore Zoo's two polar bears, turned green! The color change was caused by harmless algae growing in the bears' hollow hair shafts, and was the result of Singapore's tropical climate. Both bears were successfully bleached with hydrogen peroxide.

WALKING OCTOPUS

Scientists in California have discovered an octopus that appears to walk on two legs! A species of the tiny tropical octopus has developed a technique whereby it wraps itself up into a ball and then releases just two of its eight tentacles so that it can "walk" backwards along the ocean floor.

CRAZY GATOR

An albino alligator at Blank Park Zoo in Des Moines, Iowa, turned pink when it became excited!

ROOSTER BOOSTER

Melvin the giant rooster just can't stop growing. At 18 months old, he stood 2 ft (60 cm) tall and weighed more than 15 lb (6.8 kg)—twice as much as other Buff Orpingtons.

His owner, Jeremy Goldsmith of Stansted, U.K., said: "We're staggered. No one's heard of a cockerel this big."

MIXED PARENTAGE

Nikita the foal earned her stripes soon after her birth in Morgenzon, South Africa, in 2004. Her mother, Linda, was a Shetland pony and her father, Jonny, was a zebra!

SWIMMING FOR DEER LIFE!

At a wildlife refuge in Georgia, Rangers saw a 13-ft (4-m) alligator that had attacked an adult deer and carried it off, swimming with the animal in its mouth!

PAW PRINTS

A talented tabby cat named Bud D. Holly, who lived with Sharon Flood at her art gallery in Mendocino, California, had a number of his paintings exhibited in 1992. Twenty of the works, created with paws and watercolors, were sold, some fetching over $100.

LARGE LITTER

Tia, a Neopolitan blue mastiff from the village of Manea in the U.K., gave birth to an amazing 24 puppies in January 2005. Four puppies died shortly after birth, but the remaining 20 were more than a handful—the puppies had to be bottle-fed every four hours! Fully grown the dogs will stand 2 ft (0.6 m) high.

FLYING DOG

Star of the 2002 Great American Mutt Show, held in Central Park, New York, was Rhoadi, a small brown dog who flew through the air on a bungee cord, reaching heights of more than 6 ft (2 m). Another contest at the show, which was open to only mongrels and strays, was for the dog that was the best kisser!

SNIFFER RAT

Gambian giant pouch rats are used to sniff out deadly landmines in Mozambique. The rats are trained to associate the smell of explosives with a food reward and indicate the potential danger to their handlers by frantically scratching the earth.

FLYING SNAKE

Believe it or not, there is a snake that flies! The little-known U.S. Navajo flying snake has lateral wing-like membranes running down its body, enabling it to glide through the air.

SCARY CREEPYCRAWLY

This enormous cockroach is an amazing 3 in (7.6 cm) long and weighs 1¼ oz (35 g). Found in Brisbane, Australia, in 1997, it now holds permanent residence at the Queensland Museum.

HAPPY SHOPPER

We've all heard of dogs that fetch newspapers or slippers. Well, J.C., a golden retriever from Penn Hills, Pennsylvania, goes a step further. He regularly fetches prescriptions for his owners, Chuck and Betty Pusateri, from a nearby drugstore.

TWO-NOSED DOG

There is a rare breed of dog in the Amazon basin that has two noses. The double-nosed Andean tiger hound was first described a century ago but, in 2005, an expedition led by British adventurer John Blashford-Snell came nose to noses with a specimen. Not surprisingly, the dogs are valued for their excellent sense of smell, which they use to hunt jaguars that prey on villagers' cattle.

BIG MOUTH

The North American opossum can open its mouth wider than 90 degrees when trying to scare away an attacker.

WELL-GROOMED

A Denton, Texas, firm called Groom Doggy offers tuxedos, bow ties, and wedding dresses for our canine friends. In fact the company has everything a dog could ever want to fulfill its formal-wear needs.

MY LITTLE PONY

Even miniature horses expect to reach a height of 3 ft (1 m) or more, but Peanut, the miniature dwarf stallion, stands just 20 in (51 cm) tall. He owes his diminutive stature to his mother, who was only 26 in (66 cm) tall.

BAMBOO CAST

Malai, a 98-year-old female elephant in Thailand, broke her leg in June 2005. Her trainers put a bamboo splint on her front leg in the hope that she would fully recover.

LEGAL ROOSTER

Charged with raising poultry without a permit, David Ashley appeared in court in Seneca Falls, New York, carrying a rooster. When the judge ordered the bird to be removed, Ashley replied that it was his attorney!

DUAL-SEX CRAB

In May 2005, a fisherman caught a blue crab in Chesapeake Bay, Virginia, that was female on one side and male on the other. Females have red-tipped claws, while males have blue—but this crab had one of each. Experts at the Virginia Institute of Marine Science said the crab was an extremely rare creature called a bilateral gynandromorph, meaning it is split between two genders. They said that the crab's condition probably resulted from a chromosomal mishap shortly after its conception.

DIVING PIG

Meet Miss Piggy, the amazing diving pig! Miss Piggy jumped into the record books in July 2005 when she dived 11 ft (3.3 m) into a pool from a platform 16 ft (5 m) high at Australia's Royal Darwin Show. Owner Tom Vandeleur, who had been training Miss Piggy for a month leading up to the show, said: "She does everything herself. She goes up the 16-ft (5-m) ramp herself, she dives herself."

REGULAR CUSTOMER

One of the best customers at The Chocolate Moose restaurant in Farmland, Indiana, is Missy Jo, a 60-lb (27-kg) bulldog. Even though she never actually sets foot inside the place, Missy Jo sits outside on the patio with owner Tony Mills for a daily treat of plain cheeseburgers and vanilla milkshakes!

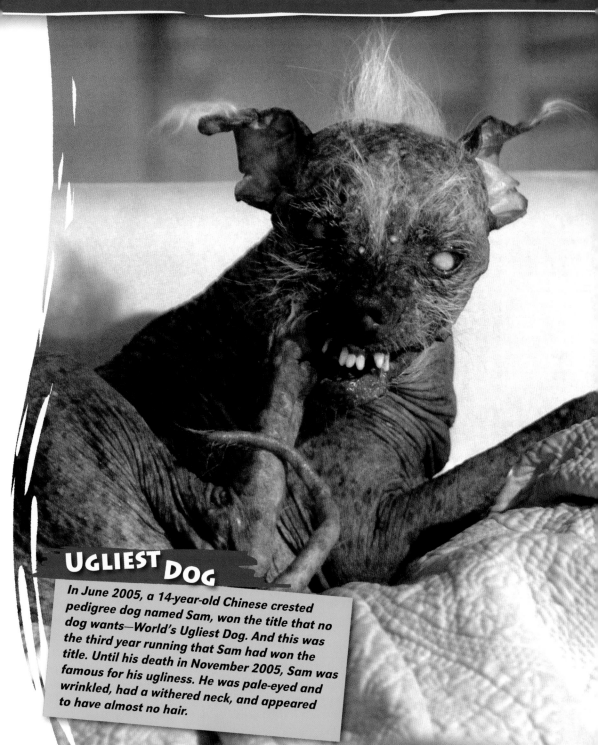

UGLIEST DOG

In June 2005, a 14-year-old Chinese crested pedigree dog named Sam, won the title that no dog wants—World's Ugliest Dog. And this was the third year running that Sam had won the title. Until his death in November 2005, Sam was famous for his ugliness. He was pale-eyed and wrinkled, had a withered neck, and appeared to have almost no hair.

STILL LIFE

Californian taxidermist Tia Resleure, stuffs animals to create fairytale worlds where pigeons wear ball gowns, chickens tell fortunes—and even kittens are framed!

IN DEPTH

How did you get the idea to create art from dead animals?

"As a child I felt closer to our pets and farm animals than to my own family. I read *Alice in Wonderland* and wanted to morph into an animal. I inherited my grandfather's collection of taxidermy from Australia, where he grew up, and my father was always picking up bones—he once made a headdress out of a zebra head."

How did you learn how to create the animal art?

"I started using animal remains in my sculptures in the early eighties, but in 1998 I went on a two-week taxidermy course just to see if I had the nerve to work with fresh specimens."

What was the first piece you ever did, and do you have a favorite now?

"On that course, I did the "Mallard on a Circus Ball" and the "Fortune Telling Chicken." The director of the school mocked me and said it was unnatural. I didn't think there was anything natural about a conventional duck flying against a piece of driftwood! My favorite piece is 'Little Shrill Voices,' which uses fetal kittens from a cat that had to undergo an emergency pregnancy spay."

What inspires your work?

"Old European curiosity cabinets, and French, German, and Russian fairy tales. When I'm working on my pieces, I imagine little stories for them."

Where do you get the animals you use?

"Because of my work in the animal welfare community, I have a lot of contacts with hobby and livestock breeders. Nothing is killed for my work— I just recycle animals that have already died."

Have you ever taxidermied your own pets?

"Yes. Part of the process of dealing with the loss of my pets is doing something with their remains. The first one I did was my first Italian greyhound, Aissi. I had to keep her in the freezer for about three years before I could start. The first time I pulled her out of the bag to let her thaw, my heart just clenched up. But then it all just went away and became very peaceful."

Do you have a future project you'd love to do?

"I have a huge old doll's house that I want to fill with animals. I want to fill the lowest level with moles, then ground-level animals on the next floor up, and little birds in the attic."

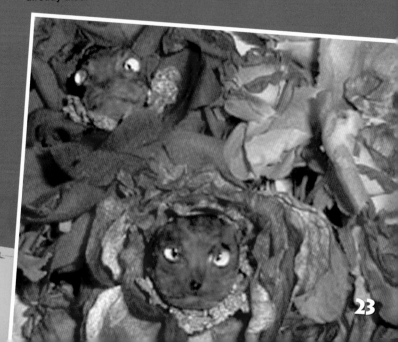

CAT CALL

After receiving an emergency call, police smashed down the door of a house in Auckland, New Zealand, in 2005—only to find that the call had been made by the homeowner's cat! The cat, named Tabby, had managed to contact the police while walking across the phone.

OPPORTUNITY KNOCKS

A bear in Croatia has learned how to trick householders into letting him into their homes by knocking at the door. Experts think that the 490-lb (222-kg) brown bear learned the ruse while nudging at a door in an attempt to get it open.

BURIED ALIVE

Thoughtful elephants in Kenya frequently bury sleeping hunters under leaves and piles of branches, thinking that the humans are dead.

TREE-CLIMBER

Ted, a four-year-old terrier, could climb 10 ft (3 m) up a tree and retrieve his ball. He was owned by Bill Vandever from Tulsa, Oklahoma.

MORE THAN A MOUTHFUL

Auggie was a dog who liked to do tricks with tennis balls. His owner Lauren Miller demonstrated his trick of picking up five tennis balls in his mouth at the same time!

DEADLY STRUGGLE

A 73-year-old Kenyan grandfather reached into the mouth of an attacking leopard and tore out its tongue to kill it. Farmer Daniel M'Mburugu was tending to his crops near Mount Kenya in June 2005 when the leopard leaped on him from long grass. As the leopard mauled him, M'Mburugu thrust his fist down the animal's throat and gradually managed to pull out its tongue, leaving the beast in its death throes. Hearing the screams, a neighbor soon arrived to finish the leopard off.

SNAPPED BACK

Cooper, a five-year-old golden retriever, managed to fight off a 14 ft (4.3 m), 700 lb (318 kg) alligator in a canal near Lake Moultrie, South Carolina, in June 2005. The dog was swimming across the canal when the reptile—three times Cooper's size—pounced. Cooper lost a few teeth and some skin, but the alligator retreated after being bitten repeatedly on the snout. Cooper's owner, Tom Kierspe, said afterward: "We've changed the dog's name to Lucky."

MONKEY BUSINESS

In Phoenix, Arizona, the SWAT team announced plans in 2005 to train a small monkey as a spy. The capuchin monkey will wear a bullet-proof vest, video camera, and two-way radio, and, intelligence experts hope, be able to access areas that no officer or robot could go.

MUDDY SWIM

For his act "Becoming Earthworm," performance artist Paul Hurley of the U.K. spent nine days in the mud and rain wearing only swimming trunks and goggles.

FISH SLAP

Marcy Poplett, of Peoria, Illinois, was injured and knocked off a personal watercraft on the Illinois River after a silver carp leaped out of the water and smacked her in the face!

UN-BEE-LIE-VABLE

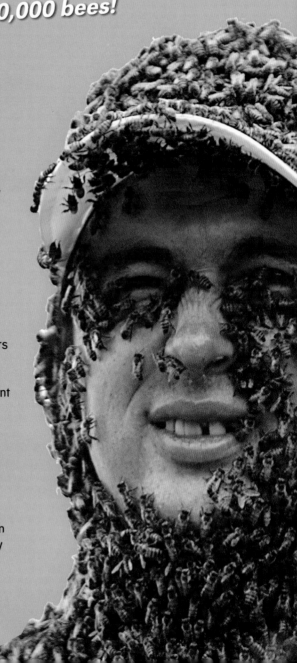

Marin Tellez created a buzz around the Colombian city of Bucaramanga in September 2005 when he covered his entire body in 500,000 bees!

Wearing just a cap and shorts, and no protective chemicals, the 35-year-old beekeeper allowed the aggressive Africanized bees to swarm all over him for two whole hours.

Once the queen bee had landed on Tellez, the rest of the colony followed on behind her, guided by her scent. Spectators were kept 30 ft (9 m) from the platform to avoid being stung, while other beekeepers stood by wearing protective suits and carrying smoke canisters in case of emergency.

Tellez explained: "I have been working with beehives for 23 years and I know how bees behave. I have to be very calm to transmit that serenity to them and to prevent them from hurting me."

He claims to have been stung so many times that his body has built up some resistance to the potentially lethal formic acid. His worst experience was being attacked by more than 150 bees when he was just 17 years old. On that occasion he saved himself by jumping into a water tank.

Tellez claims that the key to his success was, perhaps unsurprisingly, staying very calm! The bees, he says, picked up on this, and just went about their ordinary business.

Once the queen bee had landed on Tellez, the other 499,999 followed, coating the beekeeper's entire body with their swarm.

SKATEBOARDING DOG

Few sporting pets are more accomplished than Tyson the skateboarding bulldog. Tyson, from Huntington Beach, California, skates every day and is able to get on the board unaided. He runs with two paws on the tarmac and uses the other two to steer his skateboard. Then, as soon as he reaches a decent speed, he jumps aboard properly and skates for his life.

MILLI-MAGIC

Capuchin monkeys use an unusual natural mosquito repellent—they rub themselves with millipedes.

FREAK FETUS

A two-headed moose fetus, which measured about 1 ft (30 cm) long, was discovered in Alaska in 2002 after the animal's mother had been shot by a hunter.

GREAT SURVIVOR

Talbot, a six-month-old stray cat, wandered into a car plant at Ryton, England, in 1999, and went to sleep in the body shell of a Peugeot 206 on the assembly line. With the cat still asleep inside, the shell then went into the paint-baking oven at a temperature of 145°F (63°C)! Amazingly, he survived, although his paw pads were completely burned off and his fur was singed.

LITTER-KWITTER

No more unpleasant messy litter trays with the Litter-Kwitter, the ingenious invention that trains household cats to use the same toilet as their owners. Three disks slide into a seat-like device that can be positioned on the toilet bowl. The red, amber, and green disks have progressively larger bowls with smaller amounts of cat litter in them to help the cats adjust to using their owner's toilet.

FRIENDS REUNITED

Seven years after going missing from her Florida home, Cheyenne the cat was reunited with owner Pamela Edwards in 2004—after being found 2,800 mi (4,500 km) away in San Francisco.

PIG OLYMPICS

In April 2005, thousands of Shanghai residents trotted out to a city park to watch a herd of miniature pigs compete in what organizers called the "Pig Olympics."

Piglets race down a track, jostling and jumping for key positions in the hurdle race.

The pigs, a midget species from Thailand, begin training soon after birth and can start performing when they are a year old. They learn to run over hurdles, jump through hoops, dive into water, and swim—in fact, these amazing sporting pigs can do almost anything... except fly.

Two piglets compete in the swimming race.

PETS' SEND-OFF

In 1997, Patrick Pendville started the first Belgian pets funeral service. Animatrans, as it is known, offers transport, burial, individual or collective certified cremation, collection of ashes, taxidermy, facial masks, and urns. About 1,200 animals pass through the doors every year. His customers bring not only cats and dogs, but other animals such as birds, goats, horses, and sheep—and even exotic breeds, such as crocodiles, tigers, snakes, and monkeys.

FIVE-LEGGED FROG

In August 2004, nine-year-old Cori Praska found a five-legged frog with 23 toes near Stewartville, Minnesota. Three of the frog's legs appeared normal, but the fourth had another leg as an offshoot, with its own three feet attached to it.

BACK TO WORK

At the start of the 20th century, when sheep still grazed in New York's Central Park, a collie named Shep had the job of controlling the flock. When Shep was retired he was sent to a farm 40 mi (64 km) away in upstate New York. However, the determined dog quickly escaped and, even though he had never previously been beyond Manhattan, managed to find his way back to the Big Apple by first stowing away on a ferry that would take him to Manhattan Island, and then sniffing his way back from 42nd Street to Central Park!

HEALING PAWS

In the 1980s, Jane Bailey, of Lyme Regis, England, owned a cat named Rogan that was said to have healing powers. By "laying paws" on his patients' bodies, the cat was apparently able to cure sufferers of arthritis and back injuries. He became so famous that up to 90 people a week sought his help. His fur, which was combed daily, also possessed special properties and Jane would send parcels of it to those in need.

LONG TREK

In 1923, Bobbie the collie became separated from his family on a visit to Indiana. Lost and alone, he returned to the family home in Silverton, Oregon, six months later, having walked a staggering 2,800 mi (4,500 km) across seven states!

GORILLA TALK

Born in 1971, Koko the gorilla has appeared in *The New York Times* and on the cover of several prestigious magazines. Three books have been written about her, and scientists hang on her every word. She has even had her life story told on TV. For Koko, who lives at the Gorilla Foundation in Woodside, California, can communicate with humans. The 35-year-old primate has been taught sign language since she was an infant by Dr. Francine (Penny) Patterson and has now mastered more than 1,000 words. In addition, she understands around 2,000 words of spoken English and has a tested IQ of between 70 and 90 on a human scale where 100 is considered normal. Koko has also learned to use a camera and loves the telephone.

PARROT BANNED

In November 1994, a defense lawyer in San Francisco, California, wanted to call a parrot to the witness stand in the hope that the bird would speak the name of the man who killed its owner. However, the judge refused to allow it.

HAIRY HORSE

An extraordinary horse from California had a 14-ft (4.3-m) mane and 13-ft (4-m) tail.

HELPING HOOVES

Shoppers in Raleigh, North Carolina, have been witnessing some unusual sights around town—namely miniature horses, 24 in (61 cm) tall, wearing sneakers and warm blankets. These horses are the equine version of guide dogs and are being put through their paces in busy shopping malls. Janet and Don Burleson began training mini horses to help blind and visually impaired people in 1999.

MINI CAT

A blue point Himalayan cat from the U.S.A. called Tinker Toy was just 2¾ in (7 cm) tall at the shoulder and 7½ in (19 cm) long–about the size of a check book.

BABY-DRY DIAPER

Dr. Kobi Assaf, of Jerusalem's Hadassah Hospital, once treated a 12-month-old baby boy who survived a venomous snake bite because the boy's diaper absorbed the venom.

TRUMPET TUNES

Thailand's elephant orchestra has 12 jumbo elephants playing oversized instruments! Their last CD sold 7,000 copies in the U.S.A. alone.

COMPUTER BLIP

In 1988, Mastercard sent a letter to Fustuce Ringgenburg, of Hemet, California, with the offer of a $5,000 credit limit, unaware that Fustuce was in fact the family cat.

GREAT TREK

In 1953, Sugar, a Persian cat, trekked 1,500 mi (2,414 km) from Anderson, California, to Gage, Oklahoma, after her owners had moved there. The family had left the cat with a friend because of her bad hip, but despite the injury Sugar made a 14-month journey to be reunited with them.

CAT ON A HOT TIN ROOF

Torri Hutchinson was driving along the highway near Inkom, Idaho, in 2005 when a fellow motorist alerted her to the fact that her cat was on the car roof. Hutchinson, Torri's orange tabby, had been clinging to the roof for 10 mi (16 km). Torri hadn't even noticed the cat when she stopped for gas!

KISS OF LIFE

When one of Eugene Safken's young chickens appeared to have drowned in a tub in 2005, the Colorado farmer saved the bird by giving it mouth-to-beak resuscitation! After swinging the chicken by the feet in an attempt to revive it, he blew into its beak until the bird began to chirp. The farmer said: "I started yelling, 'You're too young to die!' And every time I'd yell, he'd chirp."

DÉJÀ VU

A Canadian sailor and his dog were rescued from the same island twice in a week in May 2002. Melvin Cote was hoping to spend the summer in the Queen Charlotte Islands, British Columbia, but severe weather capsized his boat. After the rescue, Cote and his dog sailed back to the shipwreck to salvage their things, but sank again in the same spot!

KENNEL OF LOVE

The doggy love motel, complete with a heart-shaped mirror on the ceiling and a headboard resembling a dog bone, opened in August 2005 for loving doggy couples. Billy and Jully, two Yorkshire terriers, stayed at the pet motel in Sao Paulo, Brazil. The air-conditioned room has a paw-print decorative motif, special control panels to dim the lights, romantic music, and films that can be screened. The rooms cost 100 reais ($54) for two hours.

LANGUAGE PROBLEM

A customer at a pet shop in Napierville, Quebec, threatened to report the shop to the Canadian government's French-language monitoring office in 1996 after being shown a parrot that spoke only English.

SHARK ESCAPE

Dolphins rescued four swimmers off the New Zealand coast by encircling them for 40 minutes while a great white shark swam nearby!

EQUINE ALLERGY

Teddy the horse has to sleep on shredded newspaper, because he has an allergy to, of all things, hay! If the horse is exposed to hay or straw, he immediately starts coughing and sneezing in an equine version of hay fever. His owner, Samantha Ashby, from Coventry, England, also has to damp down his feed to remove any dust spores.

TRENDY TERRIER

New York boutique-owner Heather Nicosia ensures that her Yorkshire terrier Woody is one of the most fashionable dogs in town. She makes him his own line of WoodyWear clothes and dresses him in a range of trendy outfits ranging from pajamas to Batman and Spiderman costumes.

FANTASTIC FISH

Bruce, an Oranda goldfish, measures a staggering 17.1 in (43.5 cm) from snout to tail fin! Named after the late kung fu star Bruce Lee, Bruce swims with normal-sized goldfish at Shanghai Ocean Aquarium.

FISHY KISS

In 1998, Dan Heath, of Medford, Oregon, could barely believe his eyes when he saw Chino, his golden retriever, standing over a fishpond, nose to nose with Falstaff, an orange-and-black carp. Each day, Chino sprints out to the backyard, peers into the water and waits. Within seconds, Falstaff pops up and the two gently touch noses. Heath doesn't know how or why Chino and Falstaff became friends, but it's obvious to everyone that their friendship is watertight.

YOUNG AND OLD

A baby hippo, weighing about 660 lb (300 kg), was orphaned when the Asian tsunami in December 2004 washed away his mother. Named Owen, he has been adopted by a 120-year-old tortoise, Mzee. Owen was spotted on the coast and taken to the Haller Park in Mombasa, Kenya. There are other hippos at the Park, but on his arrival he made straight for the ancient tortoise and the pair are now inseparable! Owen often lays his head on Mzee's shell to rest when he's tired.

BEAR'S BREATH

In May 2005, vets at Seneca Park Zoo, Rochester, New York, used a hammer and chisel to remove an infected tooth from the mouth of an 805-lb (365-kg) polar bear named Yukon. The tooth had been giving the bear bad breath.

RESOURCEFUL HAMSTER

Two house moves and some years after thinking they had lost their pet hamster, the Cummins family, from Edmonton, Alberta, were amazed when it reappeared. It turned out that the hamster had never actually left home but had burrowed into the sofa, using it as a nest. The animal had survived by sneaking out at night and taking food and water from the bowls of the family's other pets.

JUMBO ARTIST

The biggest draw at Taman Safari Park in Bogor, Indonesia, is Windi the artistic elephant. By holding on to the brush with her trunk, she dabs the paint on the canvas to form her own forest of colors. In her first six months at the park, the 18-year-old female created 50 paintings, many of which sold at over 20,000 Indonesian rupiahs ($2) each. Others were exhibited outside the park's restaurant.

INVISIBLE BEARS

Polar bears are so well insulated they are almost invisible to infrared cameras.

FIVE-LEGGED DOG

Believe it or not, a five-legged dog was found near a state park near Raleigh, North Carolina, in November 2003. Although it was previously unheard of for such an animal to live much past birth, this dog—a Maltese-terrier mix named Popcorn—was at least nine months old. A vet removed the extra leg because it was hampering the dog's movement, as well as another rear leg that rotated at a 90-degree angle, making it useless. The dog with five legs became a dog with only three.

INDIAN MARKING

This horse, owned by J.F. Daniel and R.L. Anderson, of Craigsville, Virginia, had a marking on its neck in the shape of an American Indian head.

FROG-LIFTER

Bill Steed, professor of Frog Psychology at Croaker College, Emeryville, California, trained frogs to lift barbells.

MOTHER'S MILK

A dog feeds two tiger cubs at a zoo in Hefei, China, in May 2005. The tigers' mother did not have enough milk to feed the cubs, so the zookeepers found a dog to act as wet nurse.

EAGER BEAVERS
Police searching for stolen money in Greensburg, Los Angeles, discovered beavers had found the money in their creek and woven thousands of dollars into their dam!

FERRET LOVER
C.J. Jones is mad about ferrets. After falling in love with an injured ferret that was brought to the animal hospital where she worked, C.J. opened her home to the furry little creatures, and in 1997 founded the "24 Carat Ferret Rescue and Shelter" in Las Vegas, Nevada. She looks after a maximun of 90 ferrets at a time and has rescued more than 1,500 so far in total.

MAYOR HEE-HAW
The small town of Florissant, Colombia, elected Paco Bell as its mayor. Believe it or not, he is a donkey!

JUMPING JACK
Jack, a six-year-old terrier, gained notoriety when he was banned from darts tournaments in a Welsh pub in 2001, because after each round he kept jumping up to the board, snatching the darts, and then running off with them. In his youth Jack could reach the height of the bull's eye (5 ft 8 in/1.73 m) with ease and would even snatch darts that had landed at the very top of the board.

SPEAKING CAT
Pala, a black-and-white tomcat that lived in the Turkish town of Konya in the 1960s, had a vocabulary equivalent to that of a one-year-old baby. His owner, Eyup Mutluturk, explained that the cat began talking after becoming jealous of the attention lavished upon the family's grandchildren and was able to speak freely in Turkish.

DOGGY BEACH

Bau Beach, north of the Italian capital, Rome, is a beach with a difference. Opened in 2000, it has been designed specially for dogs. Most Italian beaches ban dogs, but here for 5 euros ($6) they are given an umbrella, a towel, and a dog bowl, and their owners are handed a shovel to clean up any mess. After frolicking happily in the waves, the dogs can also take a shower under a high-pressured hose.

BULL CHASE

Despite six instances of human pile-ups, often injuring more than a hundred people, during the annual Running of the Bulls in Pamplona, Spain, since 1900, only 15 people have lost their lives.

BARK PARK!

Dog Bark Park is home to Toby and Sweet Willy. Toby is a 12-ft (3.7-m) statue and Sweet Willy, officially known as Dog Bark Park Inn, is a bed-and-breakfast establishment where guests can enter the body of the beagle to sleep. Alternatively, they can enjoy curling up in the cosy reading place in the dog's muzzle.

LIZARD LOUNGERS

Henry Lizardlover shares his Hollywood home with 35 lizards and takes amazing pictures of them in human poses. He loves them so much he even changed his name for them!

IN DEPTH

How long have you shared your house with lizards?
"Since 1981. I have a large house with separate rooms for the lizards—they don't live in cages so they get used to people. That's my secret."

Why the change of name?
"I changed my surname from Schiff to Lizardlover in the early eighties. I wanted to show my love and dedication to the lizards. I resented the stereotype that they are creepy-crawly and evil, and felt that by taking that name I was making myself a part of the lizard family."

How do you get the lizards to pose for pictures?
"If a lizard is calm and trusts you, it will demonstrate remarkably intelligent behavior, and will be happy to maintain these posed positions for up to an hour on furniture that he or she finds comfortable."

Do you have to train them?
"Not at all. I give them a comfortable room to hang out in, they see me come and go every day in a graceful and non-threatening way. They recognize that I am a friendly creature."

What are your favorite lizard pictures?
"A favorite is of Hasbro, an iguana I used to have, holding a guitar and singing into a microphone. There's also one of a big iguana cradling another in his arms—to portray that they can be loving to each other. My top models for postcards and calendars include iguanas Lovable and Prince Charming, and Chinese Water Dragons Larry Love, Laura Love, and Lana Love."

They pose like humans—do they behave that way too?
"I used to take some out to a parking lot to sunbathe—after 20 minutes they would walk back to my truck and get back in on their own. Hasbro used to scratch at night on my bedroom door, get into my bed, and go to sleep. In the morning this lizard, weighing 20 lb, and measuring 6 ft in length, would lie on my chest or, if it was chilly, poke his nose underneath the blanket."

Does everyone love what you do?
"Some people can't believe the lizards are real, or they say I drug them, hypnotize them, put them in the refrigerator first, or paralyze them. They say they can't breathe when they're posing—it's all untrue. They're calm and relaxed—scared lizards run around and bounce off the walls."

Could anyone do what you do with lizards?
"Not all act the way mine do. Male adult iguanas can be dangerous if they are in breeding season moods, they can confuse humans for other male iguanas and become violent. They can attack, rip flesh, or bite off a section of nose. You have to read their body language carefully."

PALE SCALES

Blizzard is an extremely rare 8-ft (2.4-m) adult albino alligator. Although a vicious predator, he's also very vulnerable.

His white skin, the result of a total lack of pigment in his body, leaves him very susceptible to sunburn. Because of this he was kept under cover in a specially designed tent while at the Maritime Aquarium in South Norwalk, Connecticut.

MINI MARVEL

Each fall, despite weighing just 0.2 oz (6 g), the ruby-throated hummingbird propels its tiny body, only 3½ in (9 cm) long, on a nonstop 500-mi (805-km) flight from North America across the Gulf of Mexico to South America.

LAP OF LUXURY

Under the terms of their owner's will, Chihuahua Frankie and cats Ani and Pepe Le Pew live in a $20 million San Diego mansion while their caregiver lives in a small apartment.

FLIGHT OF FANCY

Pigeon-lover John Elsworth, of Houston, Texas, decided to propose to his girlfriend via a message delivered by homing pigeon. But the bird got lost and took the note instead to the home of Rita Williams. Rita invited John over and they fell in love and got married.

A LOT OF LOBSTER

At the Weathervane Restaurant lobster-eating competition in 2004, Barry Giddings, of Chester, Vermont, devoured 19 lobsters in 35 minutes!

CHICKEN WALK

Twenty chickens strutted their stuff on a Japanese catwalk in the latest styles for the fashion-conscious hen. A range of clothing, by Austrian designer Edgar Honetschlaeger, caters for sizes small, medium, large, extra large, and turkey.

KANGAROO BAR

Boomer, an 18-month-old orphaned kangaroo, is fed peanuts by Kathy Noble, owner of the Comet Inn in Hartley Vale, Australia. In 2005, the baby kangaroo was found inside the pouch of his dead mother on the side of the road. After rearing, Boomer decided he liked the bar so much that he is now a regular visitor.

MONKEY BUSINESS

U.S. showbiz chimp Mr. Jiggs (who was actually female) was not everybody's favorite ape. On her way to entertain at a Scout jamboree, and accompanied by her trainer Ronald Winters, Mr. Jiggs walked into a bar at Freehold, New Jersey, wearing full Boy Scout's uniform. The shock caused customer Joan Hemmer to drop her drink, fall against a wall, and injure her shoulder. She sued Winters, but lost.

FRISBEE CHAMPION

Dog Ashley Whippet was such an accomplished Frisbee catcher that he was invited to appear at the 1974 World Frisbee Championships, which had previously been for humans only. Captivated by his display, the WFC devised a Catch and Fetch competition for dogs, of which Ashley became the first world champion. He performed at the Super Bowl and at the White House, and upon his death in 1985 he received a tribute in Sports Illustrated.

DOG GIOVANNI

Australian opera singer Judith Dodsworth is never short of an accompaniment—even if it is provided by her pet greyhound, Pikelet. Ms. Dodsworth says the canine virtuoso began copying her during rehearsals and hasn't stopped singing since. "As soon as I opened my mouth, he started singing. He's not bad but he's pretty loud and pretty high." And Pikelet's favorite composer? Pooch-ini, of course!

STRANGE BEDFELLOWS

Rattlesnakes hibernate through winter in groups of up to 1,000. Amazingly, they often share a site with prairie dogs—their favorite prey when they are not in hibernation.

ACKNOWLEDGMENTS

FRONT COVER (t/l) Erik S.Lesser, (c/l) © John Anderson – iStock.com, (sp) Stewart Cook/Rex Features; 4 (l) © John Anderson – iStock.com, (r) Stewart Cook/Rex Features; 5 (r) Erik S.Lesser; 8–9 Anna Kelly; 9 (t) © John Anderson – iStock.com; 10 Reuters/Romeo Ranoco; 11 Rex Features; 13 Reuters/Stephen Hird; 14–15 Rex Features; 16–17 M. Usher/Rex Features; 18 Reuters/Str Old; 19 Sam Barcroft/Barcroft Media; 20 Reuters/Sukree Sukplang; 21 KPA/Zuma/Rex Features; 22–23 www.aCaseofCuriosities.com; 26–27 Reuters/Eliana Aponte; 28 Stewart Cook/Rex Features; 29 Rex Features; 30–31 Reuters/Claro Cortes; 32 Reuters/Thierry Roge; 34 Erik S.Lesser; 35 Reuters/STR New; 36–37 Reuters/Claro Cortes; 38 Gary Roberts/Rex Features 40 Reuters/China Daily Information Corp-CDIC; 41 Reuters/STR New; 42–43 Westley Hargraves/Barcroft Media; 44–45 Mary Schwalm/AP/PA Photos; 46 Masatoshi Okauchi/ Rex Features; 47 Reuters/David Gray

KEY t = top, b = bottom, c = center, l = left, r = right, sp = single page, dp = double page

All other photos are from Ripley's Entertainment Inc.
Every attempt has been made to acknowledge correctly and contact copyright holders and we apologize in advance for any unintentional errors or omissions, which will be corrected in future editions.